THE BONES ARE THERE

The Bones Are

There

Kate Sutherland

Book*hug Press
Toronto

Library and Archives Canada Cataloguing in Publication

Title: The bones are there / Kate Sutherland.
Names: Sutherland, Kate, 1966– author.
Description: Poems.
Identifiers: Canadiana (print) 20200294989 | Canadiana (ebook) 20200295055
   ISBN 9781771666251 (softcover) | ISBN 9781771666268 (EPUB)
   ISBN 9781771666275 (PDF) | ISBN 9781771666282 (Kindle)
Classification: LCC PS8587.U795 B66 2020 | DDC C811/.54—dc23

Printed in Canada

The production of this book was made possible through the generous assistance
of the Canada Council for the Arts and the Ontario Arts Council. Book*hug
Press also acknowledges the support of the Government of Canada through
the Canada Book Fund and the Government of Ontario through the Ontario
Book Publishing Tax Credit and the Ontario Book Fund.

Book*hug Press acknowledges that the land on which we operate is the
traditional territory of many nations, including the Mississaugas of the Credit,
the Anishnabeg, the Chippawa, the Haudenosaunee and the Wendat peoples.
We recognize the enduring presence of many diverse First Nations, Inuit,
and Métis peoples and are grateful for the opportunity to meet and work on
this territory.

CONTENTS

PART I

Beasts of the Sea

Signal Codes

If it should be decided to sail in foggy weather
If it should be necessary to anchor
If the anchor should not hold
If you should see land
If the ship should run aground
If the ship should spring a leak
If we should become separated
If after separating we should not meet again

Hoist a pennant from the topmast and fire one gun
A wide pennant, a blue flag, a red flag, a tricolour flag
Hang two lanterns on the flagstaff
Show a light at the stern, ring bells and beat drums
Stop and fire two guns, keep on firing
Explode a cask of powder, light a fuse

The St. Paul

Topgallantsail wind, cold, cloudy
Unsteady wind and little of it. Clear
with passing clouds. Topsail wind. Light rain
Foggy. Heavy fog. Gale blowing
The officers wished to speak with us
The Captain said it was not safe to send a man
in the small yawl. We drew near and talked
through the trumpet. We changed our course
so that the two ships might not become separated
The *St. Paul* was astern of us
about ¼ mile, 1 mile, 1½ miles away
Not in sight. We beat the drum and rang the bell
hung a lighted lantern over the stern
The *St. Paul* disappeared at 10 o'clock

The Map

We were led astray by the unreliable map
Had we sailed E by N instead of SE by E
we should have reached the American mainland
in eight days. The map must have been false
We must have skipped across the so-called
Juan de Gama's land. I suspect the gentlemen
who drew up these charts obtained their knowledge
from visions. It is an easy matter to sit in a warm room
setting down on paper distorted accounts
and guesswork. If they must exercise imagination
let them keep their reveries to themselves
We did not find land there, not the least trace of it
Not birds, driftwood or seaweed. By July 14th
half our water was gone

Signs of Land

Red and white sea nettles, a large mass
of reed grass, various species of seaweed
adrift. Rock ducks and flocks of gulls
The frequent occurrence of animals
not commonly met in the open sea: sea otters
compelled by the shape of their hearts
to keep close to shore. We should have made it
in three or four days, ten at the most
had we taken advantage of the plainest signs
of nearness of land. We saw land as early as July 15th
but because I was first to announce it
and it was not clear enough to make a picture
the announcement was dismissed. Six weeks
after leaving Avacha we reached land

Observations and Collections

Of strange and unknown birds, I noted many
easily distinguished from Siberian and European species
by their bright colours. I sent my Cossack out to shoot
some rare birds. Good luck placed in my hands
a single specimen of which I remember seeing a likeness
in the latest account of the birds and plants of the Carolinas
This bird proved to me we were in America
Of fruit-bearing shrubs and plants, I met with a new
and elsewhere unknown species of raspberry. A few bushes
should be taken in a box with soil and sent to St. Petersburg
for further propagation. Dead tired, I penned descriptions
of the rarer plants I was afraid might wither. At sunset
I betook myself with what I had collected to the ship
where, to my astonishment, I was treated to chocolate

Meeting Americans

A fireplace, human tracks, a fox on the run
A cellar concealed beneath cut grass
A summer hut of hewn boards
Took: bundles of smoked fish, thongs
of seaweed, bows and arrows, a wooden basket
a shovel, a small copper-stained stone
Left: a piece of green silk, 2 iron knives, 2 smoking
pipes, a pound of leaf tobacco, 20 glass beads
The shout of human voices
Americans in sealskin kayaks
They would not accept our gifts
spat out Russian liquor
We fired two shots in the air
All these islands are uninhabited

Language Difficulties

A long speech in a loud voice
We construed it as an incantation, a prayer
or a ceremony to welcome us as friends
We assumed most cordial expressions
covered our lances, sabres, and guns
No one could understand their language
Our interpreter called to them in Chukchi and Koriak
but they could not understand him and pointed to their ears

I talked to them using an English book
that had American words with English translations
I questioned them about water
I asked them about wood

| воды | water | nibi | taangâx |
| дерево | wood | mittik | yâgaq |

Water Water

The mate was sent to the largest island to fetch water I made efforts at once to locate a watering place **He returned speedily bringing a small sample** I found several springs with good and wholesome water **We did not find it particularly good** The sailors chose the first and nearest stagnant puddle **It had a faint flavour of salt** I pointed out that by using their water the scurvy would quickly increase **Such water was always better than nothing** Its lime content would cause people to dry up and lose strength **We could at any rate use it for cooking** The answer was: 'Why, what is the matter with this water?' **We would have to continue using the supply we already had for drinking** 'The water is good, fill up with it!' **Being very sparing with it, we ought to be able to make it see us through** I ought to have been listened to in my capacity of physician **We had no time to lose** In the meantime I had found a still nearer watering place than the beloved salty puddle **We made arrangements to bring as much water as possible on board** I returned to the vessel to once more present my opinion on the bad water **We worked through the night** My opinion was again spurned **Our ship was not lying at all safely** I resolved in the future I would see to the preservation of my own self alone **Almost any southerly wind could pounce down without us being able to**

run for shelter The officers sent ashore a few barrels to be filled from the place I had indicated for their own consumption **That was why we wished to replenish our supplies of water in all haste** In the great hurry the barrels of spring water were left behind on shore

Our Ship

On this day our ship's brandy gave out. The erratic behaviour
of the naval officers began. They were on bad terms
with the Captain Commander. Against all reason
we sailed northward. We got into a slight altercation
on the subject. 'You do not understand it; you are not
a seaman.' I was called a wild man. Their intent
was to force me to inexcusable neglect of my duty
Master Khitrov left the lead on the bottom of the sea
which the common sailors interpreted as an evil omen
Their minds became as shaky as were their teeth
from scurvy. Many sharks were swimming
about our ship. No one any longer knew who should give
or who should take orders. The Captain Commander
shrugged his shoulders while looking at the land

The Sick List

The sailor Nikita Shumagin died on shore
By the will of God died of scurvy the grenadier
Andrei Tretyakov and we lowered him into the sea
Twelve, 16, 21, 24 men on the sick list. Naval
carpenter Ivan Petrov, drummer Osip Chentsov
Siberian soldier Ivan Davidov died of scurvy
Captain Commander and 32 men on the sick list
Today I became ill with the scurvy. I have such pains
in my feet and hands. We have few men to manage the ship
5 a.m. Captain Commander Bering died
Boatswain Nils Jansen, trumpeter Mikhail Toroptsov
cannoneer Ilya Dergachev, by the will of God
by the will of God, by the will of God. A day seldom passes
without our having to throw a corpse overboard

Beset by Storms

Every moment we expected destruction
Waves pounded our vessel like cannonballs
We could hear the wind rush
as if through a narrow passage, terrible
whistling. We lay buried among the waves, could not
see a fathom out into the ocean through hail and rain
No one could lie down, sit up or stand
Nobody was able to remain at his post
We could not cook, ate nothing
but burnt biscuits. Half our crew
lay sick and weak, the other half maddened
by the pitching of sea and ship. All courage
was exhausted. We were drifting
whither the raging heavens willed to send us

Shipwrecked

Our habitations are holes in the sand covered over with sails

There are no trees on the island. We have to search the beach for driftwood
and carry it on our shoulders 10 and 12 versts

We secure our food with great trouble, and such as we've found is bad
unfit for human beings

Sometimes, short of fuel, we're forced to eat our food almost raw

The winds are so strong, we can only with difficulty keep on our feet

During violent storms, men getting out of their hollows to relieve nature
may be whirled away

From September to March, we seldom saw a clear day

Earthquakes occurred three times

The scurvy hung on almost till spring

During breeding season, the sea bears turn savage. We can barely get by them
in safety. We have crossed over mountain ridges to avoid the beaches

We ran out of shoes

In spring and summer, there are heavy and continuous fogs

The weather greatly interferes with the speed of our shipbuilding

The men are in such poor condition and so undisciplined, it's not safe
to order them around

Our Medicine Chest

Our medicine chest had been miserably supplied
mostly filled with plasters, ointments, oils, none
of the medicines serviceable against scurvy
Misery and death got the upper hand on our ship
The small allowance of water, the lack of biscuits
and brandy, cold, dampness, vermin, and fright
were not the least important causes. Many couldn't eat
Black and swollen, their gums grew over the teeth

Raw dock root made the sailors' teeth firm again
Fresh spoonwort returned the use of limbs
Cow parsnips; turions of purple fireweed; roots
of angelica; beccabunga; watercress; infusions
of cranberry leaves. By holy Christmas Day
most had been restored to health

Mating Season

In the spring they come together in the human fashion

Sea
Cows especially about evening in a smooth sea. The female eludes

the male until, impatient, she throws herself upon her back

and the male rushes to pay her the tribute of his passion

Like human beings, they embrace with their arms

Sea
Otters and kiss each other. They copulate at all seasons

preserve their conjugal affection most constantly

The male does not serve more than one female

They cohabit after the human manner, female below, male above

Sea
Bears He comes up out of the sea upon her, seizes her in his arms

and indulges his passion with the greatest heat. The males

are very fond of their wives and are much feared by them

Sea
Lions They copulate like sea bears. Males hold females in great respect

and do not treat them so harshly as the sea bears do their wives

Their Young

         They keep the young before them while they feed
Sea Cows careful always to hold in the middle of the herd
         their tender little offspring

         They embrace their young with an affection
         scarcely credible. They engage in all the delightful games
Sea Otters a fond mother can play with her children. Asleep at sea
         they fold their young in their arms

         The parents love their young exceedingly
         When the father saw we were taking his pups
Sea Bears he wept as copiously as the female, flooding
         his whole breast even to his feet with tears

         They have an indifferent love for their pups
Sea Lions Mothers when asleep sometimes crush
         the young at their udders

Their Coats

Sea Cows

Its hide is more like the bark of an ancient oak
than the skin of an animal. It has no hair, only
bristles found round the mouth and under the feet

Sea Bears

When the pups are born they are covered in black fur
Males are larger and get a blacker coat than females
who become almost wholly ashy-grey

Sea Otters

The more cunning the animal, the more beautiful
its fur: very soft, thickly set, jet black and glossy
Rarely black all over, the head of the best grade of otters
is silvery-grey. The cheaper grade has yellowish fur
and the lowest, short, dirty-grey fur. Fifteen years ago
the finest skins sold for 5 or 6 rubles. Now
they sell for 25 and 30. Tails, much sought after
for caps and mittens, hold a particularly high price

Our Provision Store

The fresh meat of various sea animals is our universal physick **Our lack of provisions compels us to live off all sorts of unclean beasts** Otter flesh is our principal food **Our main food is sea otter** From the liver, kidneys, hearts, and meat we make several palatable dishes **Even if you can endure the smell of sea otter meat, it is as tough as sole leather and full of sinews** The flesh of the adult otter is much more tender than that of the seal **The seals are equally disgusting** The liver, heart, and kidneys of the young otter taste like those of a calf **We use not only the flesh but the entrails as well** The flesh cannot easily be distinguished from the flesh of an unweaned lamb **The sea bear has a very strong and revolting smell like an old goat** The meat of these animals smells like fresh white hellebore and is thereby repulsive to the taste **It requires a great effort to endure the smell and especially the taste** A smaller kind of sea bear has more tender and palatable meat **Nevertheless we use them all to keep ourselves alive** Our command can be sustained a whole week on two such animals **We also killed some young sea lions and these we regard as the best eating of all** The meat is of such exceptional quality and taste that we only wish to get hold of more **Their taste is particularly good and we felt better after eating them** The fat is like beef marrow and the meat almost like veal **We** now catch sea cows whose meat is far preferable to the creatures mentioned above Its fat is so sweet and fine-flavoured, we've lost all desire for butter Of all the foods eaten during our time on the island, the manati is the best The flesh has an excellent taste, not easy to distinguish from beef Yet we are never able to get enough of these revolting foodstuffs to nourish us We eat them gratefully The men should be given monetary compensation in consideration of the privations they endure on the island

Blue Foxes

We were far too busy killing blue foxes
knocking them down with the axe, stabbing them
The more of them we killed, the more
malevolent and audacious became the others
They bit off the noses, fingers, and toes of our dead
while their graves were being dug
If we lay down as if sleeping they sniffed at our nostrils
to see whether we were dead or alive
When a sailor urinated out the door of the hut
a fox snapped at the exposed part
They worried me when I was writing
carried away my maps, books, and ink
We were engaged in constant warfare against them
We did not care for their fine pelts

A New Epidemic

Scurvy had scarcely subsided when a new epidemic appeared
Through whole days and nights nothing but card playing
First for money. When this was gambled away, sea otters
were slaughtered only for their skins, the meat thrown away
Even the pelts were left lying if they weren't black enough
The most valuable skins are almost perfectly black. In the chase
of these animals, everyone tried to defraud everyone else
The more the nearer spring approached and hope rose
of being able to transport the skins home at great profit
I remonstrated with the officers to prohibit it, but the officers
were themselves devotees. Rebuilding of the vessel
progressed slowly. We killed upwards of 800
If the limits of our vessel had permitted
we should have killed three times more

Baggage Allowance

46 men

186 poods of baggage

40 water casks

25 poods of rye flour

22 poods of biscuits

2 poods of peas

5 poods of butter

1 barrel of salt beef

5 barrels of salted manati

900 sea otter pelts

187 bits of iron

2 jacks

2 small cannons

several hundred cannonballs

Our Blank Mercator Map

On our map we called the place Cape St. Elias since it was a long jutting tongue
        of land and it was on Elias' day that we anchored there
We called three small islands we discovered St. Mark, St. Stephen
        and St. Abraham
We called the island where we stood Archdeacon Stephen
We called that island Foggy Island
We called these islands the Schumagin Islands, the name of the first
        of our men to die, whom we buried here
We called a large volcano we sighted some distance inland St. Johannes
We called this island Bering Island after the late Captain Commander
We called this valley after Navigator Yushin who first discovered it
We called the unusual cave among the rock ruins after Adjunct Steller
We called the creek where we threw clubbed sea otters Sea Otter Creek
We called the place we killed them Sea Otter Field
We called the place from which we dragged great logs Wood Creek
We called the cliff that blocked our way the Impassable Rock
The southernmost point we called on our map Cape Manati
        that is to say Sea Cow

Steller's

Steller's Jay, Steller's White Raven, Steller's
Albatross, Steller's Eider, Steller's Sea Eagle
Steller's Sea Lion, Steller's Sea Cow

Polygala stellera, Stellera chamaejasme
Arabis stelleri, Campanula stelleri
Cryptochiton stelleri, Cryptogramma stelleri
Gymnandra stelleri, Veronica stelleri
Artemisia stelleriana, Gentiana stelleriana
Harrimanella stelleriana, Saxifraga
stelleriana

Cyclopterus Stelleri, Glyptocephalus
stelleri, Hexagrammos stelleri

Steller's Hill, Steller's Overlook, Steller's Arch
Steller Creek, Mount Steller

PART II

The Bones Are There

Its arms are the strangest feature of all. In these, the sea cow differs
from all other animals both of land and of sea

The solitaire has a small stump of a wing with a sort of bullet
at its extremity that serves as a defence. It is unlike anything
found in any other bird

An outstanding feature of the thylacine is its amazing mouth gape
When yawning, its upper and lower jaws form an almost straight line

McCrainie's Robber Frog   Golden Toad &
        Atitlán Grebe &   Gastric Brooding Frog &
Christmas Island Whiptail-Skink &   Eastern Cougar &

With these arms he swims, he walks on the shallows of the shore, he braces
and supports himself on the slippery rocks, he digs out and tears off algae
and seagrasses. With these he fights

With these the female embraces her lover and holds him, and permits herself
in turn to be held

Macquarie Island Banded Rail &   Rodrigues Ring-Necked Parakeet &
Warrah &   Jamaican Rice Rat &   Brace's Emerald &

Mount Glorious Torrent Frog   Guam Flying Fox &
      Bar-Winged Rail   American Ivory-Billed Woodpecker &
Slender Bush Wren &   Eskimo Curlew &

They never fly. They flap their wings when angry raising a great noise
like thunder in the distance

Charles Island Tortoise &   Torre's Cave Rat &   Labrador Duck &
     Darling Downs Hopping-Mouse &   Broad-faced Potoroo &

San Stephano Lizard   Navassa Rhinoceros Iguana &
      Greater Short-Tailed Bat   Mexican Silver Grizzly &
         Martinique Racer   Deepwater Cisco &

dog-faced *dasyurus*
dog-faced opossum
dog-headed opossum
bulldog tiger
greyhound tiger
opossum hyena
zebra opossum
native hyena
zebra wolf
marsupial wolf
striped wolf
Tasmanian wolf
Tasmanian dingo
Tasmanian zebra
Tasmanian tiger
Thylacinus cynocephalus
thylacine

Coues' Gadwall   Large Palau Flying Fox   Samoan Wood Rail &
       Atlas Bear   Himalayan Mountain Quail &

They do not eat all seaweeds without distinction, but especially

(1) that which has the shape of a club;

(2) that which has the shape of an ancient Roman shield;

(3) a very long seaweed with a wavy ruffle along the stalk

Caribbean Monk Seal &   Grass Valley Speckled Dace &
Pahrump Killifish &   Lake Titicaca Orestias &   Ratas Island Lizard &
St. Croix Tree Snake &   Greenland Tundra Reindeer &

They only lay but once in the year and only one egg

Cape Lion &   Cuban Red Macaw &   New Caledonian Lorikeet &
Jamaican Least Pauraqué &   Kioea &   Gould's Mouse &

Cascade Mountains Brown Wolf &   Japanese River Otter &
Ash Meadows Killifish &   Wake Island Rail &   Laysan Rail &
Arabian Ostrich &   Saudi Gazelle &

Height of the heart: 22 inches
Width of the heart: 25 inches
Weight of the heart: 34¾ lbs

Thicktail Chub &   Lord Howe Island Pigeon &
St. Lucia Giant Rice Rat &   Norfolk Island Kaka &

Cape Red Hartebeest   Southern Rocky Mountain Wolf &

Toolache Wallaby &   Bali Tiger &   Utah Lake Sculpin &

     Thylacine &   Molokai Omao &   Pink-Headed Duck &

We authorized the superintendent to give the following rewards for the destruction of noxious animals:

For every Male Hyena   5/-

For every Female Hyena with or without young   7/-

Half the above prices for Male and Female Devils and Wild Dogs

Cuban Short Tailed Hutia &   South Australian Spiny-Haired Rat &

Oregon Bison &   Kuluwarri &   Black-Fronted Parakeet &

Desert Rat-Kangaroo &   Hawaii 'O'o &

Lesser Stick-Nest Rat &   Schomburgk's Deer &   Heath Hen &

Ryukyu Wood Pigeon &   Lanai Omao &

It is very hard to catch them in the woods but easy in open places

As soon as they're caught they shed tears without crying
and refuse all sustenance till they die

Rodrigues Little Owl &   Tasmanian Emu &

Steller's Spectacled Cormorant &   Great Auk &

Pemberton's Deer Mouse &   Long Jaw Tristramella &

    Stumptooth Minnow &   Christmas Island Pipistrelle &

Syrian Onager &   Darwin's Rice Rat &   Paradise Parrot &

Trap the Tiger in the following ways:

(1) Build a large cage with an entrance passage, screen it with bushes. Drag a trail leading to it with bait (intestines of a sheep or rabbits and so on). Put the bait in the cage after you have dragged the trail. Set a trip catch at the end of the passage to release a door set at the entrance when the Tiger knocks it.

(2) Drag the bait along a run and set strong springer snares on this track. The snares should be of the type which will catch the feet, not a strangling snare, as we want to get the animal alive.

    White-Footed Rabbit-Rat &   Big-Eared Hopping-Mouse &

Green and Yellow Macaw &   Rodrigues Night Gecko &

The bird must have fallen accidentally into the crack
The bird had evidently fallen into a cleft
and been unable to extricate itself
The bird perhaps sought refuge there in bad weather
and was unable to get out again
The bird must have fallen into the hole
The only conjecture that can be made
is that the bird fell into the hole

New Zealand Grayling   Barbary Lion &

Red-Moustached Fruit Dove &   Grand Ilet Ameiva &

Rodrigues Day Gecko &   Indefatigable Galapagos Mouse &

In the winter the animals become so thin that all the ribs show

In the winter they are often suffocated by the ice that floats about the shore and are cast upon the beach dead

Mascarene Parrot &   Dwarf Emu &   Kittlitz's Thrush &

Bonin Islands Grosbeak &   Kosrae Crake &

Texas Grey Wolf &   Delalande's Coucal &
Lord Howe Island Flycatcher &
Lord Howe Island Vinous-Tinted Blackbird &   Laysan Millerbird &

On September 7, 1936, locked outside its enclosure on a cold night, the last known thylacine died at the Hobart Zoo

It may or may not have been named Benjamin

Kusaie Mountain Starling &   Tongan Giant Skink &
Mauritius Blue Pigeon &   Oahu Omao &   Pennsylvania Bison &

Robust White-Eye &   Carolina Parakeet &   Florida Black Wolf &
Korean Crested Shelduck &   Kenai Wolf &
Mesopotamia Beaked Toad &   Passenger Pigeon &

We cannot now hope to procure a living solitaire, though every part
of the skeleton could doubtless be found in the caverns of Rodrigues

Mysterious Starling &   Norfolk Island Pigeon &
Small Mauritian Flying-Fox &

Thick-Billed Ground Dove &
    Newfoundland White Wolf &
Grand Cayman Thrush &

Laughing Owl &
    Guadalupe Storm-Petrel &
    Mexican Dace &

Starting with 1,500 at stable stage distribution in 1750 and averaging across
all life history and starvation-caused mortality rates, the models predict a
mean of one surviving animal by 1768, the year of the recorded extinction.
The median number of survivors is zero, and the maximum is six

Réunion Ring-Necked Parakeet &
Rodrigues Greater Tortoise &

Rodrigues Lesser Tortoise &
Rodrigues Parrot &   Painted Vulture &

Slender-Billed Grackle &   Bogota Sunangel &
Queen Charlotte Islands Caribou &   Huia &   Black Mamo &
Narborough Island Tortoise &   Merriam's Elk &

a fresh series of tracks
footprints & a characteristic dropping
one solitary & doubtful footprint between button grass clumps
a single blurred foot impression on a gravelly patch of hill
20 photographs of indistinct footprints
no tracks up or downstream
no tracks out on the plains
a complete absence of tracks
a tuft of hair from its shoulder or chest
a cry three times during the night

Bluebuck &   Rodrigues Solitaire &   Tahitian Sandpiper &
Steller's Sea Cow &   Yellow-Headed Macaw &

Chatham Island Bellbird &   Guadalupe Flicker &
Arizona Jaguar &   Japanese Wolf &   Molokai 'O'o &
Choiseul Crested Pigeon &   Bulldog Rat &

These bones were found at the end of a cave
These bones were found in the same cave
These bones were found in a similar cavity
These bones were found strewn on two blocks of coral
These bones were found in a fissure in the coral
These bones were found in a patch of sandy soil
These bones were found very near the surface
These bones were found in a small cave under a foot of soil
These bones were found covered by one to two feet of soil
These bones were found under about two feet of earth
These bones were found in a hole about 25 feet deep
These bones were found in the bottom of a small cave
These bones were found at the entrance to the cavern
where the darkness begins

Martinique Amazon &   Giant Moa &
High-Fronted Mauritian Giant Tortoise & Domed Mauritian Giant Tortoise &

Maclear's Rat &   Martinique Giant Rice Rat &   Piopio &
     Auckland Islands Merganser &   Long-Tailed Hopping-Mouse &
Pig-Footed Bandicoot &   Greater 'Amakihi &

In what year did you see the animal?
At what part of the island did you see it?
At what time of year?
How was the weather? Was it high or low water?
Describe how it dived. Did it disappear completely
under the water? How was its tail shaped?
Could you see the forelegs? What was its colour?
How long do you estimate the animal to have been?
What did it eat? Does seaweed occur at that place?
Could you see far over the sea
from the place where you were standing?

Puerto Rican Hutia &   Quemi &   Mauritius Owl &
Leguat's Rail &   Dodo &   Cuban Long-Nosed Nesophont &

Spiny-Knee Leaf Frog   Navassa Curlytail Lizard &
Haitian Long-Tongued Bat   Jamaican Long-Tongued Bat &
Christmas Island Musk Shrew   St. Francis Island Potoroo &

Explanations for extinction:

(1) rapid climate change;

(2) effects of humans

A third possibility is a sea otter–sea urchin–kelp trophic cascade
A precipitous decline in the sea otter population (ecological extinction)
led to an increase in the sea urchin population led to a kelp forest collapse
led to starvation of sea cows

Explanation for ecological extinction of sea otters:

(1) effects of humans

Aurochs   Puerto Rican Caviomorph   Crooked Island Hutia &
Elephant Bird   Giant Lemur &

Nevis Rice Rat   Guadalupe Rufous-Sided Towhee &

Saint Kitts Puerto Rican Bullfinch &

Oahu 'Akepa &   Modest Rail &   Tahiti Rail &

The solitaire has never existed

The whole description is fiction

Upland Moa &   Marcano's Solenodon &   Haast's Eagle &

Malagasy Dwarf Hippopotamus &   Horned Turtle &

Guadalupe Burrowing Owl &
    Culebra Island Amazon &
Nelson's Rice Rat &

Guadalupe Caracara &
    Mamo &
Short-Tailed Hopping-Mouse &

Sighting Report Form

Location: (map coordinates, nearest reference point, altitude)
Date:
Time:
Transport: (car, foot, etc)
What was seen: (live animal, dead animal, tracks, scat, hair, fossil, call)
Observed for: (number of seconds or minutes)
If animal seen, describe its movements: (eg moving left, trotting, etc)
Where seen: (road or track, beach, paddocks, bush, etc)
Surrounding vegetation: (rainforest, gum trees, low scrub, button grass, etc)
From a distance of:
Light source: (headlights, sun, moon, etc)
Weather and visibility:
Description of animal: (head, ears, body, tail, colour, markings, length, height)
Comparison to other bush animals: (wild dog, wild cat, devil, wombat, etc)

Greater Koa Finch &   Chatham Island Fernbird &

Stephens Island Wren &   Kona Grosbeak &   Red Gazelle &

            Portuguese Ibex &   San Clemente Bewick's Wren &

The Zoological Museums of Hamburg and St. Petersburg each boast
samples of its skin though it has been asserted that one is actually the
skin of a whale

Woolly Rhinoceros &   American Cheetah &   American Mastodon &

            Sabre Tooth Cat &   Woolly Mammoth &   Irish Elk &

Puerto Rican Conure   Santa Cruz Tube-Nosed Fruit-Bat &
ʻUla-ʻAi-Hawane &   Lesser Koa Finch &   Tristan Gallinule &
Barrington Island Tortoise &   Macquarie Island Parakeet &

Sample 1: A taxidermically preserved adult male that died at the U.S.
National Zoo in 1905. Held by the Smithsonian

Sample 2: An adult female that died in the London Zoo in 1893, stored in
an ethanol solution

Sample 3: A dried skin from an individual killed by an automobile in
Greater Kingston National Park, Western Australia. The sex of the animal
was not recorded

Sample 4: A female pouch young specimen, approximately one month old,
preserved in ethanol. Collected dead in 1909 with mother and three litter mates

Giant Beaver &   Glyptodon &   Giant Ground Sloth &
Scimitar Cat &   Giant Short-Faced Bear &   Long-Beaked Echidna &

Eastern Hare-Wallaby &   Bonin Wood-Pigeon &
Ryukyu Kingfisher &   Tarpan &   Sandwich Rail &
Hawaiian Spotted Rail &   Quagga &   Jamaican Wood Rail &

De-Extinction: Cloning

(1) Find a well-preserved specimen

(2) Extract viable DNA

(3) Create a hybrid genome

(4) Engineer and implant a living cell

(5) Raise the genetically engineered offspring

(6) Release into the wild

Australian Thunderbird &   Giant Bison &   Marsupial Lion &
Magnificent Teratorn &   Megatooth Shark &   Giant Rhinoceros &

PART III

Familiar

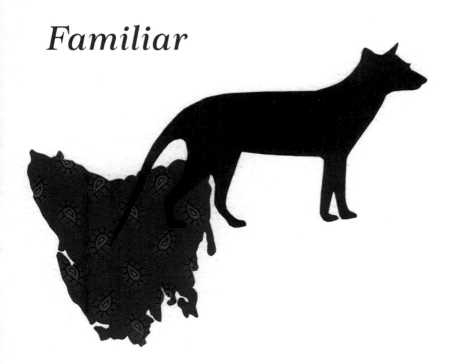

Apparatus Required:

Two or three scalpels or dissecting knives of different sizes
Two pairs of forceps, one large and one small, both straight
    with tips roughened for a firmer hold
Two pairs of scissors, one large and strong for cutting bone
    and hard tissues, the other small for fine dissections
A pair of stout needles firmly mounted in handles
A pair of the finest sewing needles mounted in handles
A metal blowpipe and a glass cannula with India rubber cap
A pocket lens with 2-3 lenses for combined magnifying power
Slides and coverslips for mounting specimens
A cheap pair of compasses for measuring
A blank notebook and an HB pencil

Spiny-Knee Leaf Frog
Phrynomedusa fimbriata

collected by Hermann Lüderwaldt
South-eastern Brazil
1898

adult female
46 mm snout to vent

known only from the holotype

tip of the snout, left tympanum
cut, incision throat to groin
exposing musculature, organs
only a very thin skin
connects femur and tibia

25 years post collection
coloration
pale blue above
reddish yellow below
iris, silver

all since faded to white

not seen in over a century
Extinct

Agnis Tompson confessed that she took a black toad, hung it up by the heels for three days, and collected the venom that dropped from it in an oyster shell. She kept the venom close covered until she should obtain a piece of linen cloth that appertained to the King: a shirt, a handkerchief, a napkin. She said if she had obtained any one piece that the King had fouled, she'd have bewitched him to death.

Executed, 1591

Kill a frog with chloroform   cut off the head with stout scissors
to make a woman tell all   she has done   take a pigeon's heart and a frog's head
dry   and reduce to powder

Sleep with me for two nights then chop off my head   at first the girl wouldn't
then she went and took an axe   and cut the head off him

A female in bad condition   a male poorly preserved   a specimen
of unknown provenance   *Fetch me an axe and chop off*
my head

Remove the skin carefully   introduce one blade of the scissors   into the cranial cavity
cut through the nerves   as far from the brain
as possible

When the steel touched him   he grew into a handsome youth   when they pushed her
into the flames   a swarm of toads burst
from the top
of her head

Mesopotamia Beaked Toad
Rhinella rostrata

collected by R. D. O. Johnson
Colombia
1914

adult male
41 mm snout to vent

eyes prominent
snout protuberant
with elongated pointed tip
tongue long, notched

body stout, large rounded
tubercles on the back, tubercles
dense on the limbs
arms slender, legs long
peculiarly large hands and feet
long, slender
fingers and toes

vocal slits present
no call observed

shaded forest floor

cover of decaying leaves
mosses and ferns
held together
by fine roots

sole adult specimen
badly faded

last seen in 1914
Extinct

Mother Waterhouse confessed she had a white cat, and willed her cat that it should destroy her neighbour's cattle, and also that it should kill a neighbour, and so it did. She kept this cat in wool in a pot, but upon being moved by poverty to occupy the wool, she prayed in the name of the father and of the son and of the holy ghost that it would turn into a toad. Forthwith, it turned into a toad and she kept it in the pot without wool.

Executed, 1566

Mount Glorious Torrent Frog
Taudactylus diurnus

collected by I. R. Straughan
Australia
1965

adult male
24.6 mm snout to vent

small, grey-brown
females cream beneath
with sparsely spotted throats
males' white, spotted throats
lack vocal sacs

dwell in streams
permanent or ephemeral
tall open forest, vine forest
fern forest, pure stands of palms

breed in warm water after heavy rain
deposit eggs
in gelatinous clumps

adults forage the forest floor
larvae, small insects

tadpoles are bottom dwellers
scrape food from the substrate
with umbrella-shaped lips

males of this species
call soft
chuckling sounds repeat
infrequent
eek-eek

last recorded in the wild in 1979
Extinct

Joan Upney confessed that a witch came to her house, gave her a toad, and told her if she owed anybody any ill will, it would go clap them if she bid it. She has never been without some toads since. She said that one day she left a toad under the groundsill at John Harrold's house, and it pinched his wife and sucked her till she died. She said that one day another toad went over her threshold as Richard Foster's wife was coming that way, and it went and pinched her. She said that her eldest daughter would never abide to meddle with her toads, but her youngest daughter would handle them and use them as well as herself.

Executed, 1589

Southern Gastric-Brooding Frog
Rheobatrachus silus

collected by David S. Liem
Australia
1972

adult male
38.4 mm snout to vent

slate-coloured
smooth, slimy skin
prominent eyes, black
with gold spots
round blunt snout
jaws close, snap

inhabit boulder-strewn
streams, spend days
submerged

summer rains initiate breeding

females swallow
fertilized eggs, tadpoles
develop in the stomach, are birthed
through the mother's mouth

fully formed froglets spew forth

1978 summer rains late
1979 rains very late
1980 & 1981 rains late again

last seen in the wild December 8, 1979
last captive frog died November 5, 1983
Extinct

Thomas Rabbet, age eight, reported that his mother, Ursula Kemp, had four spirits: the one called Tyffin, the other Tittey, the third Pigeon, and the fourth Jack. Asked what colours they were, he said that Tittey is like a little grey cat, Tyffin a white lamb, Pigeon is black like a toad, and Jack black like a cat. And he said he has seen his mother give them beer to drink and a white loaf of cake to eat. He said that in the nighttime the spirits come to his mother and suck blood from her arms and hidden places.

Executed, 1582

Daughter of a certain innkeeper
a nobleman's maidservant
the widow's eldest daughter
a witch, a female frog
conveys *ova ranarum* into an apple
offers him a most beautiful apple
warns that her imp will get into his throat
swallows her fertilized eggs
unwonted things breed in his stomach
larvae brood in the belly
a feast of toads, an abundance
of little frogs

She vomits up two lizards
and two frogs, at every word
she speaks, comes from her mouth
a snake or a toad, propulsively ejects
six living tadpoles, eight juvenile frogs
she pours the urine of a mare, newly made
on the frogs and they die
the toads were pithed, their stomachs
removed

Witches secretly learn poisons, philtres
and recipes, kept in obscurity

among old women, learned men
and philosophers forbear to mention
because the species is near
to extinction, we study only five
female frogs, many species
do not conform to the life cycle
of the common
European frog

Golden Toad
Incilius periglenes

collected by Jerry Jones, Norman Scott
& Jay M. Savage
Costa Rica
1964

adult male
44.9 mm snout to vent

marked sexual dichromism
males bright orange
females olive to black
with large scarlet spots

head wedge-shaped
eyelids warty, tongue
pyriform, not notched
voiceless

females locate males
by colour not call
each female
lays about 200 eggs

1966: 200 males visible in a 5 metre radius
1987: a normal number

1988: only 8 males & 2 females located

1989: a single male found

no sightings recorded after 1989

Extinct

Elizabeth Francis confessed she learned the art of witchcraft at the age of twelve. Her grandmother counselled her to renounce God and give of her blood to Satan, delivered in the likeness of a white spotted cat. She said every time the cat did anything for her, it required a drop of blood which she gave by pricking herself. Where she pricked herself there remained a red spot which was still to be seen. After she married, she willed the cat to lay a lameness in the leg of her husband, and it did. One morning, it lay in her husband's shoe like a toad. He perceived it when he touched it with his foot. Being suddenly amazed, he asked her what it was and she bade him kill it. He was forthwith taken with a lameness whereof he cannot heal.

Executed, 1579

A frog he would a-wooing go   thumbs thicken, rows of spines develop
along their length   *pray Mister Frog, will you give us a song?*

His daughter, a beautiful princess, the youngest brother, the little frog girl   she
made a graceful bow, became bride of the frog, married a croaking frog   she carried him
          about the forest

                    Amplex is inguinal   nuptial pads assist grip
24–36, about 200, upwards of 1100 eggs laid in strings near water   glued to rocks
     overhanging a mountain stream   spread in a thin film on the water's surface

                                                  He spreads
the eggs across her back   propels them with his feet into her pouch   holds them
in his vocal sac   carries them in her stomach   entwines them around
his hind legs

          To learn if a woman is pregnant, inject her urine   beneath a clawed
frog's skin, the motion of eggs   in women, froglets leap   from their father's
mouth   burst through the skin of their mother's back

                              The moment she deposits her eggs
the male forsakes her, he finds the frogskin and burns it   a frog
stuck with pins and buried alive will recall a faithless sweetheart
          place under his bed   a toad in a pot with its eyes sewn shut

What wonders appear in the frog only?

Scarlet Harlequin Toad
Atelopus sorianoi

collected by Enrique La Marca, Jésus
& Miguel Molinari
Venezuela
1981

adult female
with mature eggs
44.9 mm snout to vent

males are large
females larger

uniform orange-red
protruding eyes
black pupils, iris golden
tongue elongated, narrow
fingers almost free
feet, moderately webbed

inhabitants of montane
cloud forest, rich
in epiphytic plants
orchids, ferns
sloping terrain subject

to strong winds
mist, descending fog

lay egg chains
in cascading
stream

last recorded sighting 1990
presumed Extinct

Full of concern at her infant son's distemper, Dorothy Durent went to one Dr. Jacob, a man famous for curing persons bewitched. The doctor advised her to hang the child's blanket all day in the chimney corner, and at night to wrap him in it. If she saw anything in the blanket, she should take it and fling it into the fire. At night when she looked into the blanket, there fell from it a great toad which ran about the floor. A young man who was with her caught the toad and held it in the fire with a pair of tongs. Immediately it made a great noise, succeeded by a flash like gunpowder, followed by a report as great as that of a pistol. After this, the toad was no more seen. A niece of Amy Duny came to her the next day and told her Amy was in a sad condition, her face scorched with fire. She went immediately to Amy Duny and saw her face, legs, and thighs much scorched. She asked Amy how she came in that condition and Amy answered *I might thank you for it, you were the cause of it. But you will see some of your children dead, and go on crutches yourself.* She said further that since the burning of the toad, her child was well and yet alive.

Executed, 1662

The grunting of a pig   a hen cackling   the bleat of a sheep
the low bellow of an ox   a cricket singing near a stream
a dog's bark   a duck quacking   young crows cawing
a delicate insect-like tinkle   a broken banjo string
a finger running over the small teeth of a comb
a squeaky door slowly opened   a carpenter's hammer
the tapping of paddles on the side of a canoe   a cough
a watch being wound   a nasal snarl
a low-pitched snore   two marbles struck together
sleigh bells   the clangour of a blacksmith's shop

P-r-r-r   pip-pip-pip-pip   poo-poo-poo-poo-poo-poo
purrrreeeek   cr, cr, cr   cre-e-e-e-e-e-p, cre-e-e-e-e-p
pst-pst-pst   queenk, queenk   eeek!   kraw, kraw, kraw
jwah, jwah   ah, ah, ah, ah   krack, krack, krack
ca-ha-ha-ac, ca-ha-ha-ac, ca-ha-ha-ac   pé-pé, pé-pé
kle-kle-kle-klee   cran, cran, cran, c-r-r-en, c-r-r-en
creck-creck-creck   cut-cut-cut-cut   ric-up, ric-up, ric-up
ru-u-u-ummm ru-u-u-ummm   grrruut-grrruut-grrruut-grrruut
grau, grau   gick, gick, gick, gick   tschw, tschw, tschw
wurrk, wur-r-r-k   trint-trint   tr-r-r-onk tr-r-r-onk, tr-r-r-onk!

The call of this species has not been recorded

McCranie's Robber Frog
Craugastor chrysozetetes

collected by James McCranie, Kenneth Williams
& Larry Wilson
Honduras
1984

adult male
41.3 mm snout to vent

dark olive brown
with pale olive blotches
throat, venter, pale purple
palms and soles
purple

rounded canthus, iris grey
with rust-coloured horizontal bar
hidden tympanum
paired vocal slits
nuptial pads
expanded discs on fingers
and toes

found in wet forest

alongside Quebrada del Oro
stream of gold

no recorded sightings since 1994
Extinct

About midsomer last, Olive Barthram fell out with Joan Jorden and devised to afflict her with witcheries. First Olive sent three toads to trouble Joan in her bed, not suffering her to rest. The first, being tossed out into the middle of the chamber, returned and sat croaking on her bedside until thrown from the window. Within a few days another came and vexed her and it was taken and burnt. After came the third which Joan was counselled to burn herself. Going downstairs to do so, she was violently flung to the foot of the stairs and lay there a while for dead. Simon Fox put the toad into the fire and when it began to burn, a flame arose where the toad lay when Joan fell. The flame grew so great that it seemed to them to endanger the house, yet no hurt was done.

Executed, 1599

Kihansi Spray Toad
Nectophrynoides asperginis

collected by K. M. Howell & P. M. Kihaule
Tanzania
1997

gravid female
containing 16 embryos
19.8 mm snout to vent

falls plunge
into pools surrounded
by steep rock walls
fine silt, thick spray
club moss, ferns
low-growing grasses

found clambering over
damp rock outcrops
concealed in mat
of spray-soaked herbs

small
mustard yellow
eyes protuberant, pupils
elliptical, snout truncate

broadly-webbed fingers
and toes taper
at tips

yolky eggs retained
in the oviduct, fully formed
miniature toadlets emerge
through the vent

not seen or heard since 2004
Extinct in the Wild

Johan Cooper confessed she has three familiars: two like mouses, the third like a frog. The names of the two like mouses are Jack and Prickeare; the name of the third like a frog is frog. She said that she sent one of her imps to kill a child of Thomas Woodward which her imp did kill within a fortnight after. And she said that she sent her imp called frog to kill two of John Cartwright's children which her imp did kill within a fortnight or three weeks after. And she said further that at another time she sent her imp frog to destroy the wife of one George Parby and it did kill her within three days after.

Died in jail awaiting trial, 1645

fragmentation of forest

clearance of cloud forest

movement of the cloud layer up the mountainside

timber harvesting

landslides

ice in the montane grasslands

late rains

severe dry seasons

drought-related increases in evaporation

successive fires extending deeper into the rainforest

slash-and-burn agriculture

cattle grazing

illicit crops

irrigation practices

illegal mining

guerrilla activities

construction of a dam upstream

construction of a cable car

pesticides used in maize farming upstream

airborne pollution

conversion of habitat into a golf course

Las Vegas

invasion of mist flower

introduction of the bullfrog

non-native trout

safari ants

feral pigs

lack of genetic diversity

heavy parasite loads

exportation for the pet trade

stress due to handling for data collection

overcollecting

chytridiomycosis

chytridiomycosis

chytridiomycosis

Place on a slide a small drop of blood from the heart of a frog

Prick the tip of your finger and place a small drop of blood

Sources

Beasts of the Sea: "The Log Book of Bering's Vessel, the 'St. Peter,' and of Her Successor, the Hooker 'St. Peter'" (trans. F. A. Golder) in F. A. Golder, *Bering's Voyages: An Account of the Efforts of the Russians to Determine the Relation of Asia and America, Volume 1* (1922); "Steller's Journal of the Sea Voyage from Kamchatka to America and Return on the Second Expedition, 1741-1742" (trans. Leonhard Stejneger) in F. A. Golder, *Bering's Voyages: An Account of the Efforts of the Russians to Determine the Relation of Asia and America, Volume 2* (1925); Georg Wilhelm Steller, *De Bestiis Marinis, or, The Beasts of the Sea* (1751) (trans. Walter Miller & Jennie Emerson Miller, 1899); Sven Waxell, *The Russian Expedition to America* (trans. M. A. Michael, 1952).

The Bones Are There: *The Voyage of François Leguat of Bresse, Volume I* (ed. Samuel Pasfield Oliver, 1899); J. Caldwell, "Notes on the Zoology of Rodrigues" (1875) *Proceedings of the Zoological Society of London* 644; James A. Estes et al., "Sea Otters, Kelp Forests, and the Extinction of Steller's Sea Cow" (2016) 113 *Proceedings of the National Academy of Sciences* 880; Barton W. Evermann, "A Skeleton of Steller's Sea Cow" (1893) *Science* 59; Charles Y. Feigin et al., "Genome of the Tasmanian Tiger Provides Insights into the Evolution and Demography of an Extinct Marsupial Carnivore" (2018) 2 *Nature Ecology & Evolution* 182; David Fleay, "On the Trail of the Marsupial Wolf," (1946) 63 *The Victorian Naturalist* 129; G. Jenner, *Report on the Remains of the Solitaire Found in the Caverns at Rodrigues in the Months of January and February* 1871; Web Miller et al., "The Mitochondrial Genome Sequence of the Tasmanian Tiger"

(2009) 18 *Genome Research* 213; T. Mortensen, "On the 'Solitaire' of the Island of Rodriguez" (1933) 22 *Ardea* 21; Alfred Newton & Edward Newton, "On the Osteology of the Solitaire or Didine Bird of the Island of Rodriguez" (1869) 159 *Philosophical Transactions of the Royal Society of London* 327; David Owen, *Tasmanian Tiger: The Tragic Tale of How the World Lost Its Most Mysterious Predator* (2003); Leonhard Stejneger, "Contributions to the History of the Commander Islands No. 2: Investigations Relating to the Date of the Extermination of Steller's Sea-Cow" (1884) 7 *Proceedings of United States National Museum* 181; Georg Wilhelm Steller, *De Bestiis Marinis, or, The Beasts of the Sea* (1751) (trans. Walter Miller & Jennie Emerson Miller, 1899); Hugh Edwin Strickland & Alexander Gordon Melville, *The Dodo and Its Kindred* (1848).

Familiar: *A True and Exact Relation of the Severall Informations, Examinations, and Confessions of the Late Witches* (1645); *A Tryal of Witches at the Assizes Held at Bury St. Edmonds for the County of Suffolk on the Tenth Day of March 1664; The Apprehension and Confession of Three Notorious Witches* (1589); *The Examination and Confession of Certain Witches at Chelmsford in the County of Essex* (1864); Heidi Anne Heiner, ed., *The Frog Prince and Other Frog Tales from Around the World* (2010); George Lyman Kittredge, *Witchcraft in Old and New England* (1929); A. Milnes Marshall, *The Frog: An Introduction to Anatomy, Histology, and Embryology* (1882); *Potts's Discovery of Witches in the County of Lancaster* (1714); Reginald Scot, *The Discoverie of Witches* (1584); King James I, *Daemonologie* (1597).

Acknowledgements

The poem sequence "Beasts of the Sea" was published as a chapbook by knife|fork|book in 2018. Thank you to Kirby for giving my beasts their first home, and for all of the inspiration and community that kfb provided throughout the writing of this book.

Thank you to Hoa Nguyen in whose magical weekly workshops many of these poems began.

Much gratitude to the Banff Centre for the Arts, the Retreat for Writers at Hawthornden Castle, and Sage Hill Writing for providing me with time and space and gorgeous landscapes in which to write. Particular thanks to Sandra Ridley, Sylvia Legris, Steven Heighton, and Phil Hall for generous guidance and encouragement in Sage Hill poetry workshops.

And thanks again to Sandra Ridley, whose editorial brilliance made all the difference in the final stages.

Finally, gratitude always to Jay and Hazel Millar and the rest of the Book*hug team.

photo credit : Eric Bridenbaker

KATE SUTHERLAND was born in Scotland, immigrated to Canada as a child, and grew up in Saskatoon. She studied first at the University of Saskatchewan, then at Harvard Law School. She is the author of two collections of short stories, *Summer Reading* (winner, Saskatchewan Book Award for Best First Book) and *All in Together Girls*, and the poetry collection, *How to Draw a Rhinoceros* (shortlisted for a Creative Writing Book Award by the Association for the Study of Literature and the Environment). Her stories and poems have appeared in various magazines and anthologies including *Best Canadian Poetry* and *Best American Experimental Writing*. She has done residencies at Hawthornden Castle in Scotland and at the Leighton Artist Studios in Banff. She lives in Toronto where she is a professor and conducts research in the fields of Tort Law, Feminist Legal Theory, and Law and Literature at Osgoode Hall Law School, York University.

COLOPHON

Manufactured as the first edition of
The Bones Are There
in the fall of 2020 by Book*hug Press

Edited for the press by Sandra Ridley
Copy edited by Stuart Ross
Type + design by Ingrid Paulson

Cover and interior cover art is untitled
collage work by Kate Sutherland.
The three collages that appear throughout
the text are from a series
of postcard collages by Kate Sutherland
titled *Wish You Were Here*:
page 1, *Wish You Were Here #1:*
Steller's Sea Cow, Bering Island;
page 27, *Wish You Were Here #2:*
Rodrigues Solitaire, Rodrigues; and,
page 53, *Wish You Were Here #3:*
Thylacine, Tasmania. Used with permission.

bookhugpress.ca